O

STEP-UP
HISTORY

Famous Scots

Rhona Dick

Evans

Published by Evans Brothers Limited
2A Portman Mansions
Chiltern Street
London W1U 6NR

© Evans Brothers Limited 2007

Produced for Evans Brothers Limited by
White-Thomson Publishing Ltd,
Bridgewater Business Centre,
210 High Street,
Lewes, East Sussex BN7 2NH

Printed in Hong Kong by New Era Printing Co. Ltd.

Project manager: Ruth Nason

Designer: Carole Binding

Consultant: Dr Raymond McCluskey, Faculty of
Education, University of Glasgow

The right of Rhona Dick to be identified as the
author of this work has been asserted by her in
accordance with the Copyright, Designs and
Patents Act 1988.

British Library Cataloguing in Publication Data

Dick, Rhona
    Famous Scots - (Step-up history)
    1. Scots - Biography - Juvenile literature
    2. Scotland - Biography - Juvenile literature
    3. Scotland - History - Juvenile literature
    I. Title
    920'.0411

ISBN-13: 978 0 237 532055

ISBN-10: 0 237 532050

Picture acknowledgements:

Bridgeman Art Library: pages 12 (Edinburgh
University Library, with kind permission of the
University of Edinburgh), 13 and cover, top left
(Scottish National Portrait Gallery); Corbis: pages
14b (Bettmann), 20l (Phil Schermeister), 20r
(Images.com), 21 (Bettmann), 22 (Hulton-Deutsch
Collection), 23b (Hulton-Deutsch Collection); Mary
Evans Picture Library: pages 1, 10, 19t; National
Trust Photo Library/John Hammond: page 14t;
Popperfoto: pages 24, 25; Science Photo Library/
Planetary Visions Ltd: page 17b; www.scran.ac.uk:
pages 6 and cover, bottom left (Royal Commission
on the Ancient and Historical Monuments of
Scotland), 8 (Urban Archaeological Trust), 9
(National Museums of Scotland), 15 (Architecture
on Disc), 16 (The Writers' Museum, Edinburgh),
17t (The City of Edinburgh Council), 18 (Andrew
Carnegie Birthplace Museum); Topfoto: pages 7,
[11, 19b, top right], 23t, 231, 2[ ] and cover,
[ ]
M[ ] lines by Car[ol]e Binding.

Contents

Introduction

In this book you will find out about thirteen famous Scots who have made great contributions to the ways of life of others, in Scotland and beyond. They come from different periods of history and different backgrounds. For example, David I and Mary, Queen of Scots were of royal birth. Andrew Carnegie came from a much humbler home.

Changing times

The people are presented in chronological order, as shown on the timeline here. Can you think why there seem to be so few people of influence in the first 1,000 years? As you learn about the lives and achievements of these people, try to notice changes that have taken place through time, for example in ways of work, transport and the lives of women.

Who should be included?

Some of the names will be well known to you, but probably some are unfamiliar and you might be surprised at who is not included! On some pages you will find a timeline showing the names and dates of other significant Scots who lived and worked in the same era.

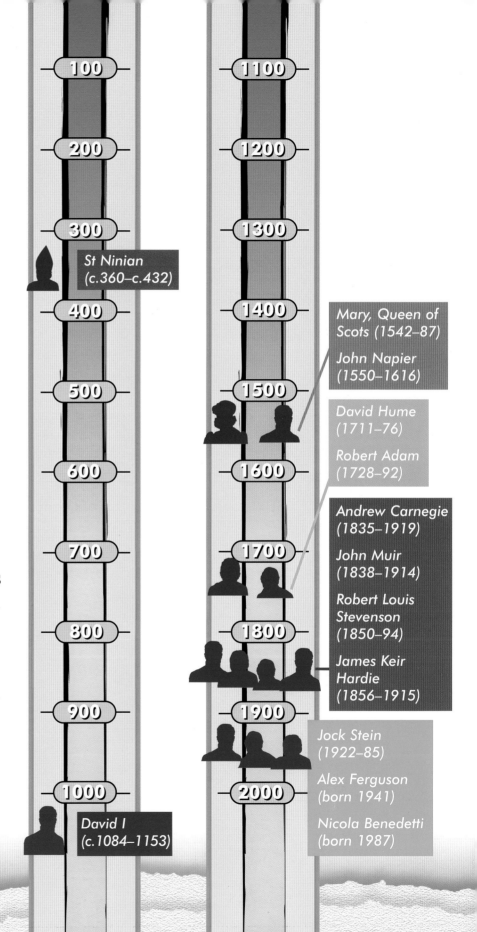

100
200
300
St Ninian (c.360–c.432)
400
500
600
700
800
900
1000
David I (c.1084–1153)

1100
1200
1300
1400
Mary, Queen of Scots (1542–87)
John Napier (1550–1616)
David Hume (1711–76)
1500
Robert Adam (1728–92)
1600
Andrew Carnegie (1835–1919)
1700
John Muir (1838–1914)
Robert Louis Stevenson (1850–94)
1800
James Keir Hardie (1856–1915)
1900
Jock Stein (1922–85)
Alex Ferguson (born 1941)
2000
Nicola Benedetti (born 1987)

Try to find out more about some of these people, and think how their work affected the lives of ordinary people in their own time and later. When you have finished reading this book, think about other famous Scots you have heard of throughout history. Who would you have included in this book?

Scotland and beyond

All the people in this book were born in Scotland but few lived their entire lives there. You will see that, as they travelled, they experienced new ideas which influenced their lives and work.

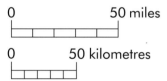

0   50 miles

0   50 kilometres

▼ *This map shows all the places in Scotland that are mentioned in this book. Perhaps you could make a class display with biographies of famous people linked to places on a map.*

SHETLANDS

ORKNEYS

Elgin

Turriff

Aberdeen

Montrose

SCOTLAND

Dundee

Iona

Stirling Dunfermline

Glasgow Falkirk   Dunbar

Clyde Rutherglen Edinburgh

Govan Hamilton

Irvine   Roxburgh

Ayr   Peebles

Dumfries

Whithorn

ENGLAND

THE BRITISH ISLES

SCOTLAND

N. IRELAND

IRELAND

WALES ENGLAND

St Ninian of Whithorn (c.360–c.432)

Ninian played an important part in spreading Christianity through the land that is now Scotland. At this time the people in different parts of the country belonged to different tribes with different languages.

Historians think that Ninian was probably the son of a king, who ruled the southwest region that is now Galloway.

Ninian was a Christian, who went to Rome to study to become a monk. He probably made the overland part of this long journey on foot. In 395 he was made a bishop.

On his way home he stayed at an abbey at Tours, in France. Here the bishop, Martin of Tours, encouraged him and became his friend. Shortly after Martin's death, Ninian returned to Scotland and built a stone church at Whithorn in honour of his friend.

▼ *This timeline shows that Ninian was one of the first Christian missionaries in the British Isles. The title 'Saint' (St) was often used for Christians who led a very good life, or who died for their beliefs. In dates, 'c.' stands for 'circa', a Latin word for 'about'.*

◄ *This is a copy of a wall painting of St Ninian, which was found in an old church in Turriff, Aberdeenshire.*

St Ninian
(c.360–c.432)

597:
St Augustine arrives in England to convert the Anglo-Saxons to Christianity.

c.563–97:
St Columba from Ireland preaches in Iona.

c.518–603),
St Kentigern (c.518–603), missionary in Scotland.

St Martin of Tours (c.316–c.397)

St Patrick (c.386–c.461 or c.491), missionary in Ireland.

From c.80 to 410, the south of Scotland is part of Britannia, a province of the Roman Empire.

c.388–410: Roman army leaves Britain.

100   200   300   400   500   600   700

Ninian's missionary work

Ninian travelled through much of Scotland, preaching the Christian message to the Celtic tribes. These included the Picts, and so he may have spoken their language.

Near Whithorn he ordered a monastery to be built, the first in Britain. Some of the monks who trained there went to Ireland and influenced the lives of St Patrick and, later, St Columba. Others continued Ninian's work in Scotland, travelling as far as the Shetlands, perhaps before St Columba arrived on Iona.

How do we know about Ninian?

Ninian lived at a time when few people could write and so details of his life could only be passed on by word of mouth. Think why this might not be reliable.

Two written sources mention Ninian, but both come from many centuries after his death. A monk called Bede (673–735) wrote that Ninian was 'a most reverend and holy man'. St Aelred (1110–67) spent some years at the court of the Scottish king David I and later wrote Ninian's life story. He says that Ninian brought stonemasons from Tours to build his church. Aelred also tells of Ninian's

▲ Ninian was buried at his church at Whithorn, which was somewhere near this spot. It became a place of pilgrimage. Robert Bruce and Mary, Queen of Scots both went there.

miracles. In one, Ninian restored the sight of a blind king. In another, he made vegetables grow instantly in a monastery garden.

What would be different?

It is almost impossible to give exact dates for events this long ago. There is confusion about when St Patrick died and recently some historians have suggested that St Ninian may have lived a century later than has been believed. Which details of Ninian's life story could not be true if he lived 100 years later?

David I (c.1084-1153)

The medieval king David I introduced many measures to improve the lives of the people of Scotland. He came to the throne in 1124.

As a child, he was sent to England and lived there for about thirty years. The first Norman kings were ruling England at this time and David learned to respect Anglo-Norman ideas. He took many of these ideas with him when he returned to Scotland as king.

Protecting Scotland

David understood that Scotland needed a strong army, to stop invaders such as the Vikings from Scandinavia. He invited Norman knights to form the basis of his army, because they were well trained, and he rewarded them with lands along Scotland's border with England. These knights and their descendants provided protection for Scotland for centuries.

The importance of trade

David realised that it wasn't enough to protect his kingdom. Trade was also important. In his reign, burghs were given the right to hold markets and fairs, and standard silver coins were minted to encourage further trade.

▼ *An artist's impression of a medieval market. David realised that Scotland would become more wealthy if trade was encouraged.*

A walk through the market

Imagine you are walking through this market. Write or record a description of everything you might see, hear, smell and feel.

David established a series of Royal Burghs, with more privileges than burghs. These were mainly ports, whose inhabitants were encouraged to trade overseas. Many developed into large and important towns.

Some of the early Royal Burghs were Aberdeen, Dundee, Edinburgh, Dunfermline, Elgin, Montrose, Peebles, Roxburgh, Rutherglen and Stirling. Find them on the map on page 5. Why do you think so many are on the east coast of Scotland?

David and the Church in Scotland

David's mother, Queen Margaret, was deeply religious, and David also had a strong faith. He was present when St Mungo's Cathedral was consecrated in Glasgow in 1136, and he established fifteen monasteries in the border areas. Many monks from Europe came to live there and brought modern Christian ideas with them. These hard-working, educated men helped to add to Scotland's wealth and provided schooling for the people.

David believed that all his subjects should be educated, although such ideas are not always practical. Why might it be difficult for poorer people to get an education? David also tried to make sure that all his subjects had the right to justice, whether they were rich or poor.

▶ This is how St Aelred (1110–67) described King David.

a gentle, just, chaste and humble ruler, loved for his gentleness, feared for his justice.

▼ Find out about some of the other famous Scots shown on this timeline.

800

Kenneth I (died 858)

900

1000

1100

▲ David I, c.1084–1153. This silver penny with his image was minted at Roxburgh.

1200

Robert Bruce (1274–1329)

William Wallace (executed 1305)

1300

John Knox (1505–72)

1400

Mary, Queen of Scots (1542–87)

1500

9

Mary, Queen of Scots (1542-87)

For many people Mary, Queen of Scots is famous because she was beheaded. The circumstances that led to her execution are complicated. The key dates tell you some of the most important events in her life. Work out Mary's age at each of these times.

Mary's flight to England

In 1568, with many enemies in Scotland, Mary chose to flee to England. She believed that she had been wrongly deposed and that her cousin, the English Queen Elizabeth, would help to restore her throne. However, Elizabeth's advisers had no intention of letting this happen, because Mary had once stated that she was the rightful queen of

Write a news report

Use the Internet and other published sources to find out the details about the murder of Lord Darnley. Use ICT to write a newspaper account of the events. If possible, include eyewitness accounts.

Key dates	
8 Dec. 1542	Mary is born.
14 Dec. 1542	Her father, James V, dies and she becomes queen.
7 Aug. 1548	Mary leaves Scotland for France.
24 Apr. 1558	Mary and the Dauphin are married.
Sept. 1559	The Dauphin and Mary become king and queen of France.
5 Dec. 1560	The king of France dies.
19 Aug. 1561	Mary returns to Scotland.
29 July 1565	Mary marries Lord Darnley.
19 June 1566	Their son, Prince James, is born.
9 Feb. 1567	Darnley is murdered.
15 May 1567	Mary marries the Earl of Bothwell.
24 June 1567	Mary abdicates in favour of her son.
16 May 1568	Mary flees to England.
15 Oct. 1586	Mary's trial for treason begins.
8 Feb. 1587	Mary is executed.

England, too. This made her a possible threat to the English monarch and so it would be very unwise to help her! By going to England, Mary had put herself in danger.

Mary and Elizabeth

Elizabeth refused to meet Mary, because Mary had been accused of involvement in the murder of her husband, Lord Darnley. Some Scottish nobles showed letters, claiming these were evidence of Mary's guilt. However, Mary was never proved guilty or innocent. Elizabeth still refused to meet her and the cousins continued to communicate by letters.

Plots and counterplots

Some English Catholics supported Mary's right to be queen of England and several plots were hatched to free Mary and murder Elizabeth. Sir Francis Walsingham, one of Elizabeth's advisers, used spies to trap Mary into becoming involved in a plot to depose Elizabeth. Mary was brought to trial, accused of treason, convicted and executed.

> ▶ *Mary's execution, 1587. Mary had many qualities for which she should be remembered. She was trusting and generous and left her subjects free to practise the religion of their choice.*

The consequences

People in some countries protested at the execution of a queen, and in 1588 the Spanish Armada was launched in an attempt to invade England. Perhaps this was in revenge for Mary's execution.

In 1603 Elizabeth died childless. She had named Mary's son, James VI of Scotland, as her successor and so he also became James I of England. Mary is often remembered as the Catholic Scottish queen who was executed by order of the Protestant English queen. However, it was through Mary's son, James, that the Scottish and English crowns were united. Every British monarch since then has been descended from Mary, Queen of Scots.

John Napier (1550-1616)

Ask your grandparents or great-grandparents if they remember using books of logarithm tables at school. These tables of numbers are what people used, before the invention of pocket calculators, to help with difficult multiplication and division calculations. Logarithm tables were first devised by John Napier, who wrote about them in 1614.

> ▶ Napier was not only a mathematician. In fact, mathematics was just a hobby. He designed an early tank and a submarine. As a landowner, he experimented with new ways of fertilising the soil. Also, he had a great interest in theology.

Why did people need logarithms?

After the Reformation more people began to question the old belief that the Earth was the centre of the Universe. A simple telescope invented in the 1600s made it possible to study the stars and planets more closely, and a German astronomer, Johannes Kepler (1571–1630), tried to work out rules for planetary motion. However, the numbers he had to work with were enormous and so the calculations took too much time. Two hundred years later a French astronomer wrote that logarithms 'by shortening the labours, doubled the life of the astronomer'.

Napier's idea of logarithm tables also led to the development of the slide rule, a calculating device that was used by scientists and engineers until the 1970s.

David Hume (1711-76)

David Hume was one of the great philosophers of the Scottish Enlightenment. He studied law at Edinburgh University, but left without graduating. Later he applied to be professor of philosophy at both Edinburgh and Glasgow universities, but he was not appointed, perhaps because people thought he was an atheist.

Hume wrote many books about his ideas. Some were not published until after his death, for even in the 18th century it could be unsafe to express views about religion, and Hume had strong views.

Hume's fork

Hume wrote that we gain knowledge in two ways, which are like two branches of a fork.

- We can *work out* some things from what we already know. For example, we can work out that 2 + 2 = 4. These 'Relations of ideas' can only be used in arithmetic, algebra and logic.

- Some things, called 'Matters of fact', must be *experienced* by one of our senses. For example, we know that the sky is blue because we see it. We know that birds sing because we hear them.

Hume's thinking greatly influenced many people, such as the economist Adam Smith (1723–90) and Jeremy Bentham (1748–1832), a social reformer.

David Hume said that the world is a well-ordered place. He asked, if it was designed by God, then who designed God? These ideas influenced Charles Darwin when he developed his theory of evolution in the 19th century.

Changing fashion

Use the portraits of Napier and Hume to write a description of the ways in which fashion seems to have changed between about 1585 and 1766.

Robert Adam (1728-92)

Increased wealth in Scotland

In the 12th century David I recognised that foreign trade would increase Scotland's wealth. Six hundred years later, in 1707, the union of the Scottish and English parliaments created the United Kingdom of Great Britain. From then, Scotland could trade with England's colonies and trading partners and, as a result, it grew much richer over the next fifty years.

By this time the buildings in Scotland's capital city, Edinburgh, were old and cramped and some were dangerous. Rich people wanted houses that showed their importance and wealth. This enabled architects such as Robert Adam to influence the development of the city.

Influences and ideas

Robert Adam followed in the footsteps of his father and three brothers, who were all architects. Between 1754 and 1758 he studied in France and Italy, learning about different styles of building. These influenced his later designs. Buildings from the time of the Roman Empire particularly fascinated him.

Robert Adam did not only design the outsides of buildings. He also provided drawings of interior features, decoration, classical ornaments and furnishings. This is his design for part of a dining room.

Robert Adam
(1728–92)

David Hume
(1711–76)

Tobias Smollett
(1721–71)

Adam Smith
(1723–90)

James Watt
(1736–1819)

1710   1720   1730   1740

Working in England and Scotland

When Robert Adam returned from Italy, he set up an architects' business with his brothers in London. They worked on many buildings in England and Scotland. One area of London that Robert designed was called Adelphi, which is Greek for 'brothers'.

In Edinburgh, from the mid-18th century, smart residential squares were built to the north of the Castle. This area became known as the New Town. Its development took many decades and several architects, including Robert Adam, were involved.

▼ Register House is one of the buildings in Edinburgh New Town that Robert Adam designed.

▼ The 18th and 19th centuries are known as the 'Age of Revolutions' because so many changes – for example, in agriculture and technology – affected people's lives. Between about 1740 and 1790 (known as the Scottish Enlightenment) interest grew in philosophy, the arts, economics and education. The people shown in orange were engineers.

Thomas Telford

Thomas Telford was a civil engineer who designed roads, bridges, canals and aqueducts in Scotland, England and Wales. Find out about the Caledonian Canal, which he engineered. Make an illustrated map of it, showing sights you would have seen along the journey when the canal was opened.

Robert Burns
(1757–1834)

Henry Raeburn
(1756–1823)

Thomas Telford
(1757–1834)

John Rennie
(1761–1821)

John McAdam
(1756–1836)

Walter Scott
(1771–1832)

Robert Stevenson
(1772–1850)

1750   1760   1770   1780

15

Robert Louis Stevenson (1850-94)

The writer Robert Louis Stevenson was the grandson of the engineer Robert Stevenson. His family hoped that he would become an engineer too, but he suffered ill health from childhood onwards and they did not think that he was fit enough for the hard work involved. He studied law at university, to make sure that he would be able to earn a living as a lawyer if he could not make money from his writing.

▶ *Robert Louis Stevenson and his father. What tells you that this photograph was taken a long time ago? Robert was born in 1850. Estimate when this photo was taken.*

Foreign travel

Stevenson probably suffered from a disease called tuberculosis, which affected his lungs. Tuberculosis can be cured now with antibiotics, but it was not until 1928 that Alexander Fleming discovered the first antibiotic, penicillin. Before that, many people felt that poor health could be improved by moving to a warmer climate.

To improve his health, Stevenson spent much time travelling abroad, although Britain was his permanent home until his father died in 1887. His travels took him to France, the east and west coasts of America and around the Pacific. In 1890, he settled in Samoa. He thought that he felt better there than ever before.

▶ *Find out about these Scots, born in the 1800s. Who do you think has most influenced your life? Those shown in orange invented or discovered something important.*

Alexander Graham Bell (1847–1922)

John Muir (1838–1914)

John Dunlop (1840–1921)

Mary Slessor (1848–1915)

David Livingstone (1813–73)

Andrew Carnegie (1835–1919)

1810   1820   1830   1840

Where did he get his ideas?

Robert Louis Stevenson wrote many types of literature. *Treasure Island* is one of his best-known adventure stories. Some stories, for example *Kidnapped*, are set in Scotland's history. Stevenson claimed that many ideas came to him in dreams. Wherever possible he drew on his personal experiences. *A Child's Garden of Verses* is a book of poetry which gives us clues about how he spent much of his childhood ill in bed.

Stevenson also wrote books based on his travels, and many stories that drew on the culture of the Pacific Islands. He criticised the Britons and Americans for trying to exploit the islanders.

Stevenson was highly thought of in Samoa. He was given the name 'Tusitala', which means 'the storyteller'. When he died suddenly in December 1894, his body was carried up Mount Vaea for burial, by the islanders whom he called his friends.

▲ *Stevenson and his wife Fanny made friends with the people of the Pacific Islands, which lie to the east of Australia.*

Objects for a story

Telephone	Fountain pen	Bicycle with
Radio	Aeroplane	pneumatic
Electric light	Biro	tyres
Television	Steamship	Waterproof
Motor car	Postage stamp	raincoat

Find out when these were invented. Which could not feature in Stevenson's stories?

Robert Louis Stevenson (1850–94)

Kenneth Grahame (1859–1932)

J. M. Barrie (1860–1937)

Elsie Inglis (1864–1917)

James Keir Hardie (1856–1915)

Charles Rennie Mackintosh (1868–1928)

Alexander Fleming (1881–1955)

John Logie Baird (1888–1946)

1850 1860 1870 1880

Andrew Carnegie (1833-1919)

Is there a public library near you? Perhaps it is a Carnegie Library. In the 19th century a new law in the UK allowed public libraries to be created, to lend books without charge. A Carnegie Library is a public library that was built with the help of money from a fund set up by Andrew Carnegie. More than 2,500 Carnegie Libraries were built around the world, including several hundred in Britain.

Who was Andrew Carnegie?

Andrew Carnegie was the son of unemployed weavers. Like many others, they had lost their jobs because of the Industrial Revolution, when machines came to be used for work that was done before by hand. In 1848 the Carnegies emigrated from Dunfermline to America.

From this time, when he was just 13, Andrew worked in the factories near his home during the day and studied accountancy at night. His abilities were recognised and he was employed

▲ This painting shows Andrew Carnegie at the opening of the library in Dunfermline, in August 1883. It was the first Carnegie Library in Britain.

by the Pittsburgh Telegraph Office and later by the Pennsylvania Railroad Company.

Andrew realised that the telegraph and railways were means of communication that would be very important in America. He invested his earnings in modern industry such as oil and railroads, and became rich.

The steel industry

Andrew visited Britain quite often throughout his life. Here he saw a new process of converting iron to steel, which he thought would be important to industry. He used his management and accounting skills to become the most powerful steel producer in America.

He devised new methods of steel production which would cut costs and increase profits. Good communications with the rest of the country meant that he could contact buyers and move his goods around quite easily.

By now Andrew was very, very rich! Unlike many business people, he paid his employees high wages. He believed that this would encourage them to work harder and so increase his profit.

Why did he give money to libraries?

Andrew Carnegie said that it was the duty of every rich man to give away his wealth for the benefit of mankind, keeping only what was needed to look after his own family.

▲ Carnegie made his steel works so efficient that few companies could compete with him.

Design a plaque

Design a memorial plaque for a Carnegie Library. Include a picture of Andrew Carnegie and some information about how he made his money and why he gave it away.

In his lifetime he gave away $350 million. He was passionately interested in education, and believed that everyone could improve their education if they had access to libraries.

◄ Carnegie wrote: 'The man who dies rich dies disgraced.'

John Muir (1838-1914)

Yosemite Valley in California is a deep gorge whose sheer sides soar thousands of metres from the valley floor.

When John's family arrived from Scotland, they farmed in Wisconsin. John later moved to California and lived there for the rest of his life.

Wisconsin

USA

California

Have you heard of Yellowstone and Yosemite National Parks? They are two of more than 300 areas of land in North America that are protected from future development – and they were founded thanks to the ideas of John Muir, who was born in Dunbar, Scotland, and moved to America with his family when he was almost eleven years old. From his earliest childhood John loved nature and he spent his life studying and conserving it. He travelled widely and is recognised as a leading person in the conservation movement worldwide.

The Sierra Nevada

John loved to walk and climb among the Sierra Nevada mountains in California. He was overwhelmed by the beauty of Yosemite Valley and the surrounding area of meadows, forests with giant sequoias, waterfalls and glaciers. However, he became concerned about the damage that sheep-farming and cattle-farming did to mountain and forest areas and in 1876 he began to write about this in magazines.

Many people agreed with his concerns and joined the campaign to get something done to protect the environment. As a result, Yosemite National Park was established in 1890. Two years later John co-founded the Sierra Club, a conservation group that still exists today.

The President and Mr Muir

Many famous people visited John Muir to hear more of his beliefs about conservation. Among them, in 1903, was the American president, Theodore Roosevelt, who camped with John for two nights in the Sierra Nevada. During the trip John hoped to convince the president of the importance of preserving the natural habitat. In 1915 Roosevelt wrote: 'Our generation owes much to John Muir.'

No temple made with hands can compare with Yosemite.

Damming the Valley

A huge earthquake devastated San Francisco in 1906. When the city was rebuilt, reliable water supplies were needed and there was a plan to create a reservoir by building a dam and flooding the Hetch Hetchy Valley in the Yosemite Park area. John Muir and others opposed the scheme, but their pleas that water could be obtained elsewhere were ignored and the valley was flooded. Many people have since agreed that it was a mistake. Shortly afterwards John died.

▶ *Woods, trails, mountains, lakes and schools are named after John Muir. Try to explain what he was saying here.*

Persuade the president

Roosevelt wrote that Muir's 'greatest influence was always upon those who were brought into personal contact with him'. Write a dialogue between Muir and Roosevelt during their camping trip, in which Muir tries to convince the president of the importance of conservation.

James Keir Hardie (1856-1915)

Founding the Labour Party

James Keir Hardie believed that members of the working class should have their own political party to speak for their interests, and in 1888 he formed the Scottish Labour Party. He was elected to Parliament in 1892. Then in 1893 he helped to form the Independent Labour Party, which later merged with other socialist organisations to become the Labour Party. In the general election of 1906 the Labour Party won 29 seats and Hardie became its first leader in the House of Commons.

Political beliefs

Hardie held strong political beliefs, including:

- Women should have the vote.
- MPs should be paid.
- The House of Lords should be abolished.
- Rich people should pay more tax than poor people.
- This would help to pay for free schooling and pensions for the elderly.

Can you say which of these ideas have now become law?

◀ *Suffragettes campaigned for the law to be changed so that women had the right to vote in elections. Hardie agreed with them. He was once arrested at a suffragette meeting, but was released because he was the leader of a political party. It was 1928 before all women over the age of 21 could vote.*

What influenced Hardie's ideas?

Many of Hardie's socialist ideas were probably influenced by his early life. He was born to Mary Keir, a single mother, who was a servant. She later married David Hardie, a ship's carpenter, but the family was still very poor.

James never went to school, and when he was seven years old he became a baker's errand boy. When David was ill, James was the only wage earner in the family, but he lost his job for arriving late one morning. At age ten, James started work in the coal mines, working underground for twelve hours a day. He spent his evenings learning to read and write.

James was worried by the conditions that miners faced. In the 1870s he organised the miners into a trade union and arranged a strike. The mine owners were furious and James was sacked and blacklisted.

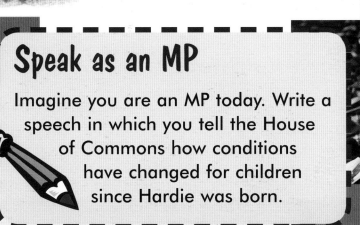

◀ *James Keir Hardie as miners' leader in the 1870s.*

To earn a living, he opened a tobacconist and newsagent's shop before beginning to write for a publication called *The Miner*. He hoped that his writing would give miners a political education. For the rest of his life Hardie worked to improve the lives of the working classes.

Other politicians born in Scotland

You could make a timeline of politicians:
Tony Blair (born 1953)
Gordon Brown (born 1951)
Sir Menzies Campbell (born 1941)
Robin Cook (1946–2005)
Donald Dewar (1937–2000)
Margaret Ewing (1945–2006)
Winnie Ewing (born 1929)
Alec Douglas-Home (1903–95)
James Ramsay Macdonald (1866–1937)
George Robertson (born 1946)
David Steel (born 1930)

▶ *In 1914 James Keir Hardie spoke at a demonstration against the First World War.*

Speak as an MP

Imagine you are an MP today. Write a speech in which you tell the House of Commons how conditions have changed for children since Hardie was born.

Two football greats

Among many Scots who have excelled in sport, there have been some outstanding footballers. Here you can compare the careers of two such famous men.

Jock Stein (1922-85)

John (Jock) Stein was born near Hamilton, Lanarkshire, in 1922. He left school at 15 and became a coal miner. In 1942 he started to play at weekends for Albion Rovers, but still worked in the mines in the week.

Jock joined Llanelli Town, a Welsh club, in 1950, earning £12 per week as a professional player. In 1951 Celtic paid Llanelli Town £1,200 for him, and the next year Jock became Celtic's captain. He remained with Celtic until the end of his playing career in 1956.

Jock managed Dunfermline from 1960 until April 1964. Then he joined Hibernian for one year, before returning to Celtic as manager in 1965. In 1978 he managed Leeds United for just 45 days, before accepting the post of Scotland's manager. Jock died suddenly, while watching Scotland play Wales in a World Cup qualifying match in 1985.

Jock Stein Record of Achievements

Date	Club	Cup	Wins	Player/Manager
1953	Celtic	Coronation Cup	1	Player
1954		Scottish Cup	1	
		League Championship	1	
1960	Dunfermline	Scottish Cup	1	Manager
1965–78	Celtic	European Cup	1	Manager
		Scottish Cup	8	
		League Championship	10	
		League Cup	6	
1982	Scotland	World Cup finals		Manager

▶ *Under Jock Stein's leadership, Celtic became the first British team to win the European Cup. Alex Ferguson often took Jock's advice on footballing matters.*

Alex Ferguson (born 1941)

Alexander Ferguson was born in Govan in 1941. After leaving school he became an apprentice toolmaker in the Clyde shipyards. He played as an amateur for Queen's Park and St Johnstone.

His first professional signing was for Dunfermline in 1964. In 1967 Rangers bought him for £65,000, but his career there was brief. He moved to Falkirk in 1969 and then to Ayr United in 1973.

Alex Ferguson Record of Achievements				
Date	Club	Cup	Wins	Player/Manager
1980–85	Aberdeen	European Cup Winners' Cup	1	Manager
		European Super Cup	1	
		Scottish F.A. Cup	4	
		League Championship	3	
		League Cup	1	
1986–	Manchester United	F.A. Cup	5	Manager
		Premiership Champions	8	
		League Cup	2	
		European Cup Winners' Cup	1	
		European Champions League	1	
		European Super Cup	1	
		Intercontinental Cup	1	

In 1974 Alex earned £40 per week managing East Stirling, but after four months he moved to St Mirren. In 1978 he was appointed manager of Aberdeen, where he stayed until he became caretaker manager of Scotland in 1985. In 1986 he joined Manchester United and in 2006 Sir Alex Ferguson was still their manager.

▼ *Although Alex Ferguson was not a great player, he is recognised as an outstanding manager. He has won more trophies for his teams than any other British manager.*

A football 'Who is Who?'

Which other people do you think should be included in a book entitled 'Who is Who in Scottish Football'? Choose two or three of them to write about for the book. Try to sum up each person's life and achievements in 50 to 100 words.

Nicola Benedetti

For the last person in this book we have chosen Nicola Benedetti. She is at the beginning of her career as a musician, but has already performed to important people in many countries. In 2004 she played before the Queen at the opening of the Scottish Parliament.

Nicola plays at a concert in London, in September 2005.

When and where were you born?	I was born in Irvine, Ayrshire, on 20 July 1987.
Why did you decide to play the violin?	My older sister wanted to learn, and my mother asked if I would like lessons, too. I cried all the way through my first lesson, but my mother encouraged me!
How old were you when you started playing?	I started having lessons at school when I was four. After that first lesson I enjoyed it and sometimes practised for three hours a day.
What happened then?	A few years later I auditioned for the Yehudi Menuhin School near London. I got a place and started there when I was ten years old. I was a bit homesick at first, but I soon began to enjoy it and played in lots of concerts. I was going to have lessons with Lord Menuhin himself, but sadly he died. He was a world-famous violinist.

Have you won any competitions?	Yes, when I was 14 I won Britain's Brilliant Prodigy Competition, and in 2004 I won the BBC's Young Musician of the Year Competition.
How did these wins affect you?	When I was 15 I decided to leave the Yehudi Menuhin School, because it was difficult to fit in my concerts in Scotland with my lessons near London. My parents weren't happy, but in the end I persuaded them that it was the right thing to do, especially as I had a tutor to continue my education.
Do you only play concerts in Scotland?	No. My diary for this year shows that, apart from concerts in Britain, I shall be travelling to perform in Germany, Japan, the USA and Canada.
Do you have a favourite violinist?	No, I like to listen to them all. Each plays in an individual way. Eventually you can recognise their style.
Are there any challenges left?	Goodness, yes! There are always new works to learn or old works to revisit. The challenge is to be well prepared, to the point where performing a piece becomes an enjoyable experience.

Timeline

Use the information on these two pages to draw up a timeline showing the events in Nicola's life up to now.

▶ *This timeline shows some famous Scots from the world of the arts. If you could interview a famous Scottish person who is alive today, what would you ask them about their future?*

Sean Connery (born 1930) — 1930

Billy Connolly (born 1942)

Lulu (born 1948) — 1940

Robbie Coltrane (born 1950)

Jack Vettriano (born 1951) — 1950

Annie Lennox (born 1954)

James MacMillan (born 1959)

Robert Carlyle (born 1961) — 1960

Evelyn Glennie (born 1965)

— 1970

Ewan McGregor (born 1971)

Paul Thomson (born 1976)

— 1980

Nicola Benedetti (born 1987)

— 1990

Glossary

abbey — a religious building where monks work.

abdicate — to give up the throne.

algebra — a branch of mathematics which uses symbols to stand for numbers.

amateur — working without any payment.

Anglo-Norman — to do with English people whose ancestors first came to England from Normandy with William the Conqueror in 1066.

antibiotics — drugs that can destroy infections.

apprentice — a young person who works with a craftsman to learn the trade.

aqueduct — a bridge that carries a canal or other water across a valley.

architect — someone who designs buildings.

atheist — someone who believes that there is no God.

audition — to perform a piece as a test.

bishop — an important churchman.

blacklist — to put on a list of names of people who might be troublemakers.

burgh — a small town holding a market or fair.

caretaker manager — someone who takes on the manager's job until a permanent manager can be found.

chronological order — a sequence from the earliest time to the most recent time.

civil engineer — someone who uses their knowledge of science and mathematics to design roads, railways, bridges, canals or other projects to benefit mankind.

classical ornaments — vases, statues, etc made in the style of the ancient Greeks and Romans.

climate — the weather that is usual in a particular country or region.

co-found — to set up something with the help of another person.

colonies — overseas lands belonging to a country.

consecrated — made holy in a special service and dedicated to God.

conserve — to keep safe or protect from damage.

Dauphin — the eldest son of the king of France.

decade — ten years.

depose — to overthrow.

economist — someone who studies the way a country uses its money.

emigrate — to leave one country to live permanently in another.

errand boy — a messenger.

excel — to be better than other people.

exploit — to take advantage of.

fertilising — adding substances that will improve the soil and feed crops.

glacier — a river of ice which moves very slowly and erodes the land it passes over.

graduate — to be awarded a degree at the end of university study.

habitat — the natural environment where animals or plants usually live.

House of Commons — the part of the British Parliament whose members are elected.

Industrial Revolution	a period in the 18th and 19th centuries when major changes took place in working practices.
invest	to lend money to a company, so it can expand and develop, in exchange for a share of its profits.
knight	a highly skilled soldier who usually fought on horseback.
logarithm tables	mathematical tables which make calculations easier to do.
medieval	from the Middle Ages, i.e. the time in history between about 400 and 1450.
mint	to make coins by stamping images and cutting them out of metal.
miracles	events that cannot happen naturally.
missionary	a person sent by the Christian Church to teach about Christianity in another place or country.
monastery	a religious building where monks live and work.
Norman	from Normandy in northern France.
parliament	a group of people who meet to make decisions and pass laws.
pension	money paid to a retired person.
philosopher	a thinker; someone who loves wisdom.
Picts	people who lived mainly north of the River Forth in what is now Scotland.
pilgrimage	a journey to an important religious place.
planetary motion	the regular orbits of the planets.
Premiership	the league of best teams in English football.
prodigy	someone, usually quite young, who shows a great skill or ability.

professional	paid for working.
Reformation	period in the 16th century when new ideas about religious practices and beliefs spread across Europe.
reverend	highly respected.
Scottish Enlightenment	a time, between about 1740 and 1790, when there was a growing interest in philosophy, the arts, education and economics in Scotland.
sequoias	giant redwood trees.
social reformer	someone who believes in changing the organisation of a community.
socialist	someone who believes that wealth should be produced by and shared among all members of the community.
stonemason	a craftsman who carves and builds with stone.
strike	a time when employees stop working to try to force their employer to improve working conditions.
suffragette	someone who campaigned for women to be given the vote.
telegraph	an early electronic method of communication.
theology	the study of religion and beliefs about God.
trade union	an organised group of workers who try to bring about improvements in working conditions for everyone.
treason	disloyalty to or betrayal of a monarch or country.
tutor	a teacher who works with one student only.

For teachers and parents

This book looks at people in the past with a Scottish focus within the five main historical eras, and is designed to develop children's knowledge, understanding and skills in History. To develop awareness of chronology, the people are presented in chronological order.

Throughout the book and in the associated activities children are encouraged to use a range of historical skills and to understand how the characteristic features of a period impact on the people involved. There are opportunities for children to make links between situations and to identify changes across different periods. Children are also encouraged to see that the people's achievements were long-term, influencing many generations in many countries.

Whilst providing guidance, the activities are designed as starting points for further research, and in every case the children should plan their work carefully, select from the information available in this book and elsewhere, and present their findings appropriately. The activities are designed principally to develop history skills, but often make links with other curriculum subjects. Children should use ICT where appropriate, particularly for research and presentation. Wikipedia (http://en.wikipedia.org/wiki/Main_Page) is a useful and generally reliable source of information on the people featured in this book. However, children should be encouraged to make sensible judgements about the accuracy of information from the Internet.

http://www.scran.ac.uk is an online learning resource service with free access for Scottish schools. It has numerous high-quality pictorial resources, including original documents.

SUGGESTED FURTHER ACTIVITIES

Pages 4 - 5 Introduction
Imagining that they are going to write a book like this, children could make a list of ten other famous Scottish people from different periods. They should name people from different walks of life, such as sport, theatre, art, politics or business, then jot down summaries of their achievements and the reasons why they should be included.

In groups, children could research and write about a theme, such as 'Scottish People in Medicine'. They should present the people chronologically and try to identify links across time periods.

Children could think about why so few women are included in this book and speculate on the gender balance if a similar book were written in the year 3000.

Pages 6 - 7 St Ninian (c.360–c.432)
Help the children to understand the difficulties of providing exact dates for events so long ago, when written records were scant.

Celtic decoration was used on memorial stones at about the time of St Ninian. The decoration is supposed to represent the unending cycle of life and death. Children could draw and decorate a Celtic cross.

Children could act out the stories of Ninian's miracles.
http://www.stbrigids-kilbirnie.com/Pages/ninian.html
http://www.seanachaidh.org/stninian.htm
http://www.fordham.edu/Halsall/basis/Jocelyn-LifeofKentigern.html

Pages 8 - 9 David I (c.1084–1153)
The youngest son of Malcolm III and St Margaret, David didn't become king until almost 30 years after his father's death. St Margaret was English, and the niece of Edward the Confessor, the last Anglo-Saxon king of England, so links with the English royal household were close.

The children could draw a family tree showing the line of descent from Malcolm III to Alexander III.
http://www.royal.gov.uk/output/Page108.asp
http://www.scran.ac.uk/sp3/PDF%20files/David%20I.pdf

Answer to question on page 9: Royal Burghs were on the east coast because this was where the main trade routes were.

Pages 10 - 11 Mary, Queen of Scots (1542–87)
Mary is an enigmatic, perhaps politically naïve, character who lived in a time of turmoil and intrigue. She had a few trustworthy advisors and supporters, but many powerful men put their own interests before loyalty to their queen. Children could research some of the influential people in Mary's life and assess the impact each had on her.

They could research Mary's childhood in France and compare her life there with her later life in Scotland.
http://www.royal.gov.uk/output/Page134.asp
http://www.learningcurve.gov.uk/snapshots/snapshot02/snapshot2.htm

Page 12 John Napier (1550–1616)
Napier studied at St Andrews, and possibly went abroad to further his scientific studies. This would have been hard before the Reformation and Renaissance, as the Church was cautious about scientific experiments. Napier was the first mathematician to adopt the use of the decimal point to separate integers and fractional parts of numbers. This made such numbers simpler to understand, calculate and record.

Children could make and use a set of Napier's bones (or rods).
http://www.macs.hw.ac.uk/~greg/calculators/napier/simulation.html.

Napier also had ideas for various weapons, including a mirror that would set fire to ships 'at whatever appointed distance', 'devices for sailing under water' and 'a chariot that would…scatter destruction on all sides.' Children could draw plans of these.

Page 13 David Hume (1711–76)

Hume has been described as the most influential Scotsman of all time. Children could suggest other Scottish people who have influenced them and give their reasons.

They could give more examples of Hume's Fork. For instance, they could write ten 'Matters of fact', providing two for each of the senses. http://www.bbc.co.uk/history/scottishhistory/enlightenment/features_enlightenment_enlightenment2.shtml

Pages 14 - 15 Robert Adam (1728–92)

The Adam brothers were famous in London for creating the Adelphi area, but the scheme almost bankrupted them. For a time Robert Adam was an MP and had to resign his post as architect to the king because MPs are not permitted to hold paid offices of the crown.

Children could look at pictures of Adam buildings and use these to help them design the frontage for a building in Charlotte Square in Edinburgh New Town. They could use similar architectural features to design a fireplace to go inside the building. See http://sites.scran.ac.uk/ada/ra.htm.

Children could investigate the careers of the great engineers of the period and write illustrated summaries of their work. http://www.icivilengineer.com/Famous_Engineers/

During the Industrial Revolution thousands of miles of canals were built. It cost less to transport heavy goods by canal than by road, since one horse could tow a barge carrying a ton or more. However, the usefulness of canals was short-lived, with the coming of the railways. Children could draw and label diagrams of how a lock works. See http://www.starling101.btinternet.co.uk/canals/lckworks.htm.

They could use Design & Technology skills to make an aqueduct that allows water to flow from one end to the other.

Pages 16 - 17 Robert Louis Stevenson (1850–94)

Stevenson is remembered mainly for his fiction and children's verse but also wrote travel books. *The Strange Case of Dr Jekyll and Mr Hyde* was based on the true story of Deacon Brodie of Edinburgh. It is not suitable for children to read, but you could tell them a bowdlerised version and they could then write their own stories based on this.

They could analyse the rhythm and rhyme pattern used in *A Child's Garden of Verses* and write poems in this style, remembering that Stevenson often based his poems on his own experiences or dreams.

To commemorate the 100th anniversary of Stevenson's travels in the Pacific, the Marshall Islands issued a commemorative stamp showing scenes from his books. The children could find summaries of his stories and design a stamp using these and a map showing where Samoa is.

Pages 18 - 19 Andrew Carnegie (1835–1919)

Discuss the meaning of 'philanthropy' and help the children to draw up a list of other philanthropists from different periods in history, such as

Cadbury, Lever and Rowntree. They could research the lives of these men and write obituaries explaining the reasons for their generosity. http://www.thoemmes.com/dictionaries/bdm_carnegie.htm http://www.scotcities.com/carnegie/intro.htm http://www.kcl.ac.uk/depsta/iss/library/speccoll/carnegie.html

Pages 20 - 21 John Muir (1838–1914)

Children could use Google Earth (download free from http://earth.google.com) to look at the results of flooding the Hetch Hetchy Valley. The coordinates of the O'Shaughnessy Dam are approximately 37° 56' 51.97'' N and 119° 47' 17.08'' W.

There are several areas named after John Muir. The children could locate some and design an appropriate plaque at the entrance.

John Muir's pioneering work in conservation in America has inspired similar work elsewhere. Children could investigate the work of the John Muir Trust (http://www.jmt.org) and suggest ways of conserving their own environment.

Pages 22 - 23 James Keir Hardie (1856–1915)

Keir Hardie first entered Parliament wearing his tweed suit and a cloth cap. Tradition dictated that he should wear a black tailcoat and top hat. Children could write a newspaper comment on his appearance.

Children could find out about the people and events of the struggle for votes for women. They could use ICT to create leaflets explaining why women should have the vote, and stage rallies in which they speak out for universal suffrage. http://scotlandvacations.com/hardie.htm http://www.scotlandspeople.gov.uk/content/help/index.aspx?r=546&1122

Pages 24 - 25 Two football greats

Discuss with the children why Jock Stein was not conscripted for war service. The children could research the subject of Bevin Boys. http://www.sundayherald.com/np/managerprofilestein.shtml http://www.manutdzone.com/playerpages/SirAlexFerguson.htm

Discuss what makes a great sportsperson: e.g. a sense of fair play, inspiring others, being a good loser. List famous sportspeople and ask the children to research their careers and make a short speech justifying the epithet 'great'.

Pages 26 - 27 Nicola Benedetti

Children could find out about other musicians who were famous when young, such as Vanessa Mae and Nigel Kennedy. From reading simple biographies of them, they could create 'interviews' like that of Nicola. See http://www.vanessa-mae.com and http://www.nigelkennedy.com.

Children could compare a day at their school with a day at the Yehudi Menuhin School. See http://www.yehudimenuhinschool.co.uk/1d.asp.

They could consider what qualities are needed to make a great musician (or artist): e.g. talent, patience, hard work. They could look for evidence of these at http://www.nicolabenedetti.com.

Index